BEACH WALK

Storey Publishing

CONTENTS

NATURE FIELD GUIDES

BEACH FUN & GAMES

SEASIDE HUNTS

DISCOVERY ZONE

Plus! **My Beach Log & Beach Patch Stickers**

Are You Ready for a Beach Adventure?

Ah, the beach. Big water, warm sand, and open sky — it's a great place to explore, learn, and have fun! Bring your curiosity and sharp eyes and ears.

THINGS TO BRING IN YOUR BACKPACK

This book and a pen or pencil

Hat and sunglasses

Beach toys

Eco-friendly sunscreen

Snacks

Towel

Water bottle

Bucket and shovel

BEACH PATCH STICKERS

There are 12 patch stickers in the back of this book that match **I SEE IT!** circles on some of the pages. When you find something in nature that matches something on an **I SEE IT!** page, put the sticker on the matching circle. See how many you can find!

Shells

A MOLLUSK IS AN ANIMAL WITH NO BONES AT ALL. Instead, many of them make hard shells to protect their bodies. As these mollusks grow, their shells slowly get bigger and bigger, making room for the animal inside. Their shells come in all sorts of different shapes, colors, and sizes.

Most snails make a single spiral-shaped shell, while oysters and clams have shells that open and close like a box!

I SEE IT!

Put your patch here

What kinds of SHELLS do you see?

Common periwinkle

Kitten's paw

Lion's paw scallop

Jingle shell

Common whelk

Auger shell

Blue mussel

Keyhole limpet

Razor clam

Moon snail

Oyster

Hard-shell clam

Cockle

River mussel

Slipper shell

Tiger conch

Look for shells that are smooth or jagged to the touch!

If you were a mollusk, what would your shell look like?

Take a LOOK

Look closely at a shell. Notice how the inside is always smooth, no matter how rough the outside is.

17

BEACH TIPS

Here are some ways to turn a day at the beach into a learning adventure.

Read the posted beach rules before you hit the shore.

Sunburns are no fun! Use sunscreen and cover up with a hat and sunglasses.

Use your senses to see, hear, smell, and touch.

Always take your trash with you!

Be aware of waves and currents in the water, and be careful walking over slippery or sharp rocks.

Only swim with an adult.

Look for wildlife, but keep a respectful distance.

Sand & Stones

I SEE IT!

PUT YOUR PATCH HERE

YOU MAY THINK ALL SAND IS THE SAME, BUT IT'S NOT! Wind, rain, ice, and waves break down rocks and minerals into the billions of tiny pieces that form sand. Because rocks differ in their color, texture, and hardness (depending on how they are formed), sand does, too.

Beach stones lose their rough edges and become smooth over time as they are tumbled in water and sand.

What kinds of **STONES** do you see?

Can you find a heart-shaped stone?

Do they feel smooth or rough?

Colored pieces of sea glass can look like stones, but they're not!

Can you find a stone with stripes or spots or swirls?

Sea glass

What color is the **SAND** at your beach?

WHITE SAND may be made of quartz or broken up pieces of coral or shells.

REDDISH-ORANGE SAND comes from minerals high in iron.

BLACK & GRAY SAND often comes from basalt, which is black lava from volcanoes.

Take a LOOK

Pick up a handful of sand. Notice how it's really made up of super tiny rocks. What different colors do you see?

SAND GAMES!

A wide-open beach is a great place to play a game. Try some of these for simple fun.

SAND DARTS

Draw three circles in the sand with a stick to make a target. Take turns tossing a stone or shell and add up points when one hits the target. You get **1 point** for the outer circle, **3 points** for the middle circle, and **5 points** for the bullseye in the center.

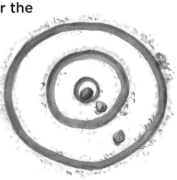

TiC-TAC-TOE

Tired of running around? Take a break and play some tic-tac-toe. Use a stick to draw your board in wet sand and make Xs and Os, or use shells and stones as markers.

HOPSCOTCH

Draw a hopscotch court on wet sand. Toss a rock onto the court. Now hop down the line, landing on one foot on single boxes and both feet on double boxes. Skip over the box with the rock on it. Hop all the way to the 10, then turn around and hop back, picking up your rock along the way.

LONG JUMP

Draw a line in the sand. Take a running start and when you hit the line, leap as far as you can! Mark where you landed and see how far your friends can jump next.

Sea Stars

I SEE IT!

PUT YOUR PATCH HERE

SEA STARS, SAND DOLLARS, AND URCHINS ARE ECHINODERMS [eh-KIE-no-derms]. Their name means "hedgehog skin" because they are covered in pointy little spines that make them rough to the touch. Most sea stars have five arms covered in tiny sucker feet that help the animal creep along the sea bottom and catch mollusks to eat.

Many sea stars can regrow a whole new arm if they lose one!

What kinds of **CREATURES** do you see?

Cushion sea star

Short-spined sea urchin

Watch out! Those spikes are sharp!

Green sea urchin

Spiny red sea star

Common sea star

Purple sea star

Spot a sea star? Count how many legs it has.

Morning sun sea star

Purple sea urchin

Washed up, dead sand dollars are often white and smooth to the touch.

Eccentric sand dollar

Keyhole sand dollar

Take a LOOK

Flip over a sea star or sand dollar and look for the small hole at the center of its body. You just found its mouth!

Build a SAND CASTLE

Nothing says a day at the beach like building a sand castle. Not into castles? Try sculpting a mermaid, an octopus, or a giant sea turtle!

USE MOIST SAND. If you can roll a ball of damp sand in your hands and it stays together, you're ready to build!

BUILD A STRONG BASE. Create a mound of sand, then add a little water and pack it down with your hands or a shovel. Slowly add more sand, then more water, and keep packing it down until you like the size and shape.

Drip castles are super easy and fun to make. Just grab a big handful of watery sand and let it slowly drip through your fingers in one spot. Create pointy mounds of different sizes.

ADD DETAILS. Create turrets and tunnels. Don't forget to dig a moat and fill it with water! Use your tools to create stairs and windows. Decorate your castle with stones, sticks, and shells. Work from the top so falling sand won't ruin your work below.

Tool tip: Spatulas, big spoons, and other kitchen utensils are good for carving details, but smooth stones, shells, and sticks work, too.

Build near the tide line, or dump buckets of water on dry sand as you go along.

Shorebirds

I SEE IT!

PUT YOUR
PATCH HERE

MANY BIRDS LIVE NEAR THE SHORE. They come in all shapes and sizes, from gulls and ducks to herons and plovers. Some have webbed feet for swimming. Some have long, pointy bills for jabbing fish in the water and finding creatures in the sand.

Greater yellowlegs sandpiper

Shorebirds often have long legs for wading in shallow water while they hunt for food.

What kinds of **BIRDS** do you see?

Oystercatcher

Ring-billed gull

Brown pelican

Osprey

Bald eagle

Can you find any birds with long legs? Or webbed feet?

Herring gull

American avocet

Great cormorant

Do you see a bird hunting for food in the sand or water?

Great blue heron

White ibis

Plover

Atlantic puffin

Take a LOOK

Find a feather? Is it a small, fluffy down feather or a long, stiff flight feather?

SANDPIPER SAYS

Follow the directions and learn more about how animals move!

HOW TO PLAY: Pick one person to be the sandpiper. The sandpiper tells the rest of the players what to do. Players only follow commands that begin with the words "Sandpiper says." If the leader shouts, "Sandpiper says bark like a seal," everyone should bark.

But if the sandpiper just says "Bark!" without saying "Sandpiper says," then nobody should bark. Any player who barks is out of the game till the next round.

Players need to listen carefully to stay in the game as long as possible. The winner becomes the sandpiper for the next round!

TRY SOME OF THESE IDEAS: SANDPIPER SAYS . . .

WAVE YOUR ARMS like an octopus.

SCOOP WITH YOUR BEAK like a pelican.

DIG like a clam.

SCUTTLE like a crab.

CHOMP like a shark.

LEAP like a dolphin.

LISTEN UP!

Close your eyes for a moment and really listen to the sounds around you. Do you hear any of these things?

☐ Wind blowing

☐ Birds calling

☐ An insect buzzing

☐ Plants rustling

☐ Waves lapping the shore

☐ Children laughing

☐ Feet walking on wet sand

What else can you hear?

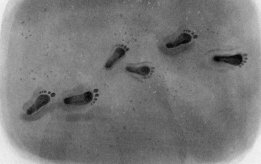

Shells

I SEE IT!

PUT YOUR PATCH HERE

A MOLLUSK IS AN ANIMAL WITH NO BONES AT ALL. Instead, many of them make hard shells to protect their bodies. As these mollusks grow, their shells slowly get bigger and bigger, making room for the animal inside. Their shells come in all sorts of different shapes, colors, and sizes.

Most snails make a single spiral-shaped shell, while oysters and clams have shells that open and close like a box!

What kinds of **SHELLS** do you see?

Common periwinkle

Kitten's paw

Common whelk

Keyhole limpet

Hard-shell clam

Razor clam

Lion's paw scallop

Look for shells that are smooth or jagged to the touch!

Slipper shell

Jingle shell

Auger shell

Moon snail

Cockle

If you were a mollusk, what would your shell look like?

Blue mussel

Oyster

River mussel

Tiger conch

Take a LOOK

Look closely at a shell. Notice how the inside is always smooth, no matter how rough the outside is.

Fun with
SHELLS & STONES

The beach is full of natural treasures! Grab your bucket, take a stroll, and see what you can find. Collect interesting stones, empty shells, or sticks. Bring them back to your beach towel and sort them in different ways.

SORT BY SIZE

Find the smallest object and place it in on the ground. Now put down the second smallest object next to it, and the third, and so on, all in a long line that ends with the biggest item.

SORT BY SHAPE

If you've collected lots of shells, put all the spiral cone shells in one pile, and all the dish-shaped shells in other pile. If your beach has more stones than shells, you can make separate piles for round rocks, flat rocks, and odd-shaped ones.

SORT BY COLOR

Divide your beach finds by color. Put white with white, green with green, pink with pink, and so on. Now arrange those piles out into lines and put them in rainbow order!

Seaweed

I SEE IT!

PUT YOUR PATCH HERE

"SEAWEED" IS THE COMMON NAME FOR UNDER-WATER PLANTS AND ALGAE THAT GROW IN OCEANS AND LAKES. Seaweed provides food and shelter for lots of aquatic animals. For example, sea otters, crabs, and many fish shelter in giant underwater kelp forests. Sea turtles, lobsters, and other animals love to snack on seaweed.

Giant kelp

If you've ever had sushi, you've probably eaten seaweed!

What kinds of **SEAWEED** do you see?

Red dulse

Irish moss

Knotted wrack

Bladder wrack

Did you find any green, red, or brown seaweed washed up on shore?

Sea palm

Gutweed

Dead man's fingers

Eelgrass

Sea lettuce

Giant kelp

Pondweed

Search for kelp air bladders that look like rubber beads!

Sugar kelp

Take a LOOK

Look and feel how slimy, thick, and rubbery seaweed is compared to the plants you find on land.

MAKE A SUNDIAL
Tell Time with Sunshine

A sundial is a kind of clock. It tells time based on where the sun is in the sky, so it only works on sunny days. To make a simple one at the beach, you need a straight stick, 12 rocks or shells, and a watch. If you do this at the beginning of your day, you'll have a better idea of how a sundial works.

1 Find a place out in the open away from any shade. Smooth out a patch of sand and push the stick into the ground so that it stands up straight.

2 Put a rock on the end of the shadow made by the stick. Check the time and set an alarm to go off in one hour. (If you want to be more exact, start the sundial on the hour, like 10 o'clock.)

3 When the alarm goes off, check where the shadow falls now. Mark that spot with another rock. An hour later, mark the shadow with another rock. Put the rest of your rocks in a circle to make a clock on the ground, spacing them the same distance apart as the first three rocks. That way you don't have to wait 12 hours to finish your clock!

4 Check your sundial before you leave to see where the shadow is falling. How many hours did you spend at the beach today?

Don't look directly at the sun — it could damage your eyes.

SMELL IT!

Explore the shore with your sense of smell. Use your nose to sniff out the scents around you. Do you smell any of these things?

☐ Wet sand

☐ Warm stones

☐ Something fishy

☐ Seaweed

☐ Wet dog

☐ Sunscreen

☐ Something sweet

☐ Something stinky

☐ Flowers

☐ Salty air

☐ Grass

☐ Damp towel

Tide Pools

TIDE POOLS ARE PUDDLES OF WATER LEFT BEHIND when ocean water flows away from the shore during low tide. Many different kinds of crabs, sea stars, snails, and other creatures live in these rocky natural aquariums. They have to hide or hold on to the rocks so waves don't wash them out to sea during high tide!

Imagine if your home were flooded all the way to the roof twice a day!

What kinds of **CREATURES** do you see?

Common gray sea slug

Breadcrumb sponge

Gooseneck barnacle

Can you spot any little crabs scuttling under rocks?

Hairy hermit crab

Periwinkle

Peanut worm

Ribbed limpet

Chiton

Acorn barnacles

Sea anemones

Limpets and barnacles stick themselves to rocks and don't move!

Moon snail

Dog whelk

Spider crab

Take a LOOK

Find an anemone? Study how it opens and closes its many armlike tentacles like flower petals waving in the water.

WATER & WAVES

You'll probably spend a lot of your beach trip looking out at the water. Notice how it is always changing and moving.

What **COLOR** is the water today?

Is it **BLUE**?

Is it **GRAY**?

Is it **DARK BLUE**?

How does the **SURFACE** of the water look?

Is it **AQUA**?

Is it **CALM**?

Is it **ROUGH**?

Are there **SPARKLES** from the sun?

Wind, underwater currents, and tides keep oceans and large lakes in constant motion.

HIGH TIDE, LOW TIDE

You can track the ocean tides throughout the day.

Push a stick into the wet sand when you get to the beach. Check on your stick during the day. Is the water moving away from it or coming closer? Your stick might end up underwater if the tide is coming in!

A **FLOWING TIDE** pushes water up on to the shore at **HIGH TIDE**.

An **EBBING TIDE** pulls it back into the ocean to create **LOW TIDE**.

The beach looks bigger during low tide because more sand shows when the water moves out to sea.

Crustaceans

I SEE IT!

PUT YOUR PATCH HERE

CRABS AND OTHER CRUSTACEANS [krus-TAY-shuns] DON'T HAVE BONES. Instead they have hard, "crusty" exoskeletons. From giant lobsters to tiny fairy shrimp, crustaceans come in lots of shapes and sizes. Many live in the ocean, but some live in freshwater or even on land. Look for crabs scuttling sideways across the sand!

Hermit crab

Most crustaceans have eyes at the ends of stalks that rise up from their heads!

What kinds of **CRUSTACEANS** do you see?

Northern shrimp

Stone crabs

Blue crab

Have you spotted any crustaceans in the water? What about on the sand?

Dungeness crab

Green crab

Hermit crabs

Goose barnacle

American lobster

Hermit crabs can't make their own shells. Instead they find empty ones to hide in.

Crayfish

Take a LOOK

All crustaceans have two pairs of antennae. Look closely and see if you can find them.

WATCH A CRAB GROW

Follow the pictures below to see how a stone crab grows from egg to adult.

A female crab releases millions of **EGGS** into the water.

An egg hatches two weeks later, and a **ZOEA [ZO-ee-yah]** larva pops out and floats toward shore.

Over the next month the zoea grows and changes into a **MEGALOPA [MEH-gah-lo-pa]** and settles down to the water's bottom.

. . . until it becomes an **ADULT CRAB**.

As the **BABY CRAB** grows, it sheds its shell several times . . .

TOUCH IT!

Use your hands to explore the beach in a new way!
Can you find and feel all these different textures?

Something **ROUGH**

Something **WET**

Something **SMOOTH**

Something **WARM**

Something **SLIMY**

Something **SOFT**

Something **PRICKLY**

Something **COOL**

Something **DRY**

Fish

I SEE IT!

PUT YOUR
PATCH HERE

NO MATTER HOW DIFFERENT THEY LOOK, ALL FISH HAVE SOME THINGS IN COMMON. They have backbones and they live their whole lives in water, breathing through their gills.

Most fish use their senses of hearing, taste, and smell to move through the water. Some chase and catch their food. Others swallow tiny plants and animals floating in the water.

King salmon

There are more kinds of fish in the world than all mammals, birds, reptiles, and amphibians combined!

What kinds of **FISH** do you see?

Seahorse

Clownfish

Atlantic stingray

Angelfish

Pufferfish

American eel

Can you spot any fish swimming in the water?

Parrotfish

Garibaldi

Sculpin

Reef shark

What is your favorite type of fish?

Bluegill

Listen for the sounds of fish splashing!

Largemouth bass

Northern pike

Rainbow trout

Take a LOOK

If you find a dead fish on shore, take a closer look. Does it have teeth? Can you find its gills? What color are its scales?

Build Some BEACH CRITTERS

Oceans and lakes are full of interesting animals. You can create your own critters using stuff you find on the beach.

1 Think of an animal that swims in the water or hangs out on shore. It could be a fish or a seabird, a seal or a shark — anything at all. You can even invent a new kind of creature that hasn't been discovered yet!

2 Look around for natural materials to use. A piece of driftwood or a rock could form the body of a turtle or fish. Seaweed makes good jellyfish tentacles or octopus arms. Shells can be used for wings or fins. Sticks and grasses make nice legs and antennae.

3 Arrange your materials on the ground. Piece them together to form your beach critter.

4 Now tell someone all about it! What does your critter eat? Where does it live? How does it move around? What does it eat? Does it have a name?

Take a photograph of your new friend, then leave your critter where you created it!

Marine Mammals

I SEE IT!

PUT YOUR PATCH HERE

MARINE MAMMALS LIVE NEAR OR EVEN IN THE OCEAN, BUT THEY AREN'T FISH. Mammals breathe air and have warm blood. They give birth to live young instead of laying eggs. Dolphins and whales never leave the water. Seals, sea lions, and sea otters spend some time on land.

Some marine mammals hunt for fish or other sea animals. Others eat very tiny animals called zooplankton [ZOO-plankton]. Manatees only munch seagrass!

A sea otter's dense fur keeps it toasty in cold water. Other marine mammals use extra fat called blubber to stay warm.

Sea otter

What kinds of **MARINE MAMMALS** do you see?

Manatee

Orca

Marine means "of the sea."

California sea lion

Did you know a group of whales or dolphins is called a **POD?**

Do you hear any seals barking?

Bottlenose dolphins

Fur seal

Harbor seal

Take a LOOK

Every person has their very own fingerprints. Take a closer look at yours. Instead of fingerprints, humpback whales have their very own tail markings!

MARINE HABITATS

Oceans and lakes have many different habitats between the shore and the deepest water. Look at the three pictures. Do any of these habitats look like the water near you? Count the animals and plants in each picture.

A **habitat** is a place where plants and animals live.

KELP FOREST

Kelp forests are underwater habitats made of giant seaweed. They provide food and shelter to sea otters, fish, crustaceans, and many other creatures.

CORAL REEF

Warm, shallow waters provide the best place for coral reefs. The reefs themselves are made of tiny creatures that grow into large formations.

SEAGRASS MEADOW

This marine ecosystem has grasslike plants growing underwater. It is home to shrimp, manatees, and many fish.

Jellyfish

I SEE IT!

PUT YOUR PATCH HERE

LOOK BUT DON'T TOUCH! If you spot a clear, blobby thing in the water or washed up on shore, be careful. It's probably a jellyfish. These animals use stinging tentacles to stun their prey before eating it. While a jellyfish won't sting you on purpose, you could still get hurt if you touch one, even if it's dead.

Sea nettle jellyfish

A **tentacle** [TEN-ta-cul] is like a finger. It's used for feeling and grabbing.

What kinds of **JELLYFISH** do you see?

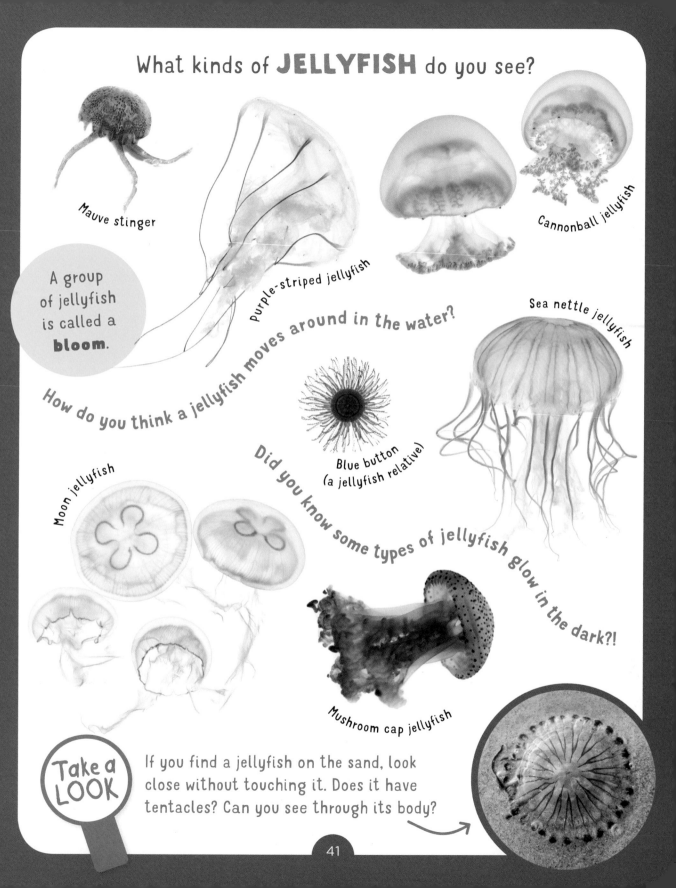

Mauve stinger

purple-striped jellyfish

Cannonball jellyfish

A group of jellyfish is called a **bloom**.

How do you think a jellyfish moves around in the water?

Blue button (a jellyfish relative)

Sea nettle jellyfish

Did you know some types of jellyfish glow in the dark?!

Moon jellyfish

Mushroom cap jellyfish

Take a LOOK

If you find a jellyfish on the sand, look close without touching it. Does it have tentacles? Can you see through its body?

Marine
MANDALAS

A mandala is a circle-shaped design with patterns in it that you can make almost anywhere out of nearly anything. It's really fun to make them outside on the ground. You can find all the supplies you need right on the beach!

1 To make your mandala, collect a bunch of shells, stones, sticks, seaweed, or sea glass. Smooth a patch of sand.

2 Arrange some of your treasures on the ground to form the center of your mandala. Now place other objects in a larger circle surrounding the center. Make as many circles or spokes as you like!

3 Your beach mandala can be as big or small, and as simple or fancy, as you want. Try making one with different colors and one using only objects of the same color.

Instead of collecting supplies, draw your design right in the wet sand with a stick!

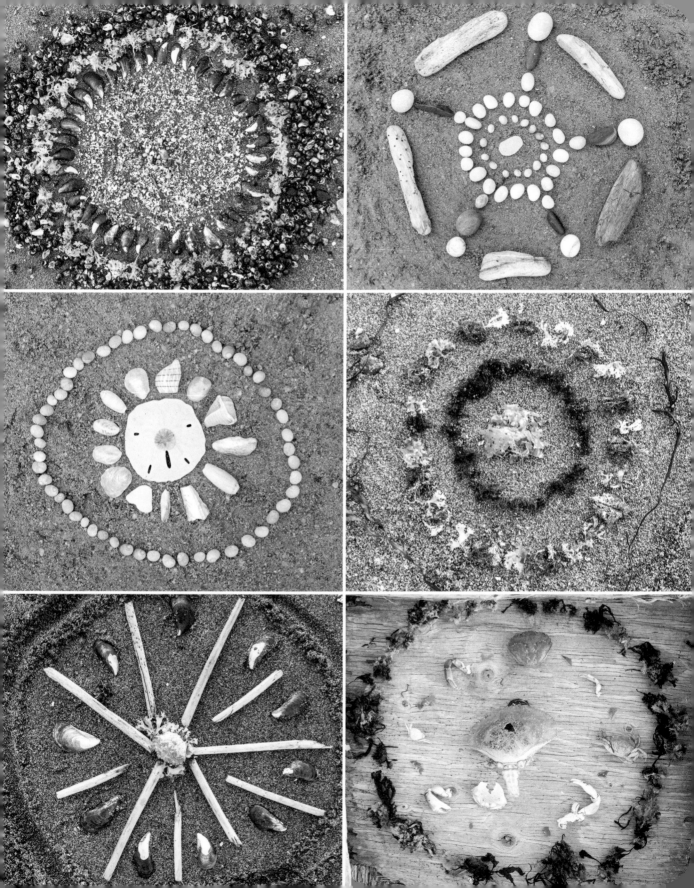

Tracks

ANIMALS LEAVE SIGNS IN LOTS OF PLACES, but their tracks (footprints) are especially easy to spot on wet sand. Studying tracks can provide clues about where an animal lives, what it eats, and how it moves. Walking birds leave individual footprints, but crabs, sea turtles, and seals leave long drag marks that look more like tire tracks in the sand.

Hermit crabs have 10 legs, but they only use 4 of them for walking.

What kinds of **TRACKS** do you see?

Gull

Crow

Duck

Heron

Try leaving a line of your own hand- or footprints in the sand!

What shape is the print? Does it have individual toes or webbed feet?

Dog

Green turtle

Snail

Hermit crab

Loggerhead turtle

There might be a nest full of buried eggs nearby!

Seal drag marks

Did you find turtle tracks?

Take a LOOK

Find a hole in the sand? Peer inside and see if you can find the edge of a clam shell or crab leg hiding down there.

45

Coastal Plants

I SEE IT!

PUT YOUR PATCH HERE

BEACHES ARE HOME TO MANY DIFFERENT SHRUBS, TREES, GRASSES, AND FLOWERS. These tough plants can withstand strong offshore winds without blowing over. Their roots help hold the sandy soil in place so it doesn't wash away. Birds, insects, and other coastal animals depend on these plants for food and shelter.

Look for insects buzzing or crawling along different beach plants.

WHAT I DID ALL DAY

Find a sticker that matches your activities!

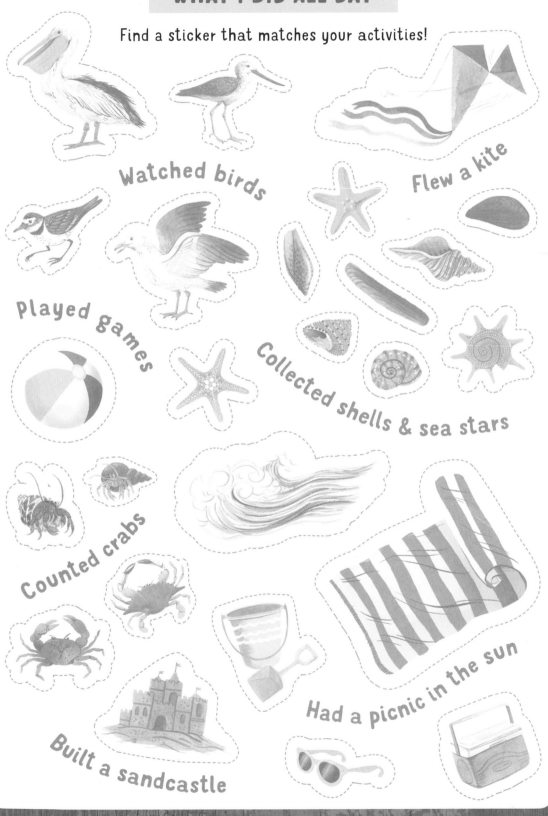

Watched birds

Flew a kite

Played games

Collected shells & sea stars

Counted crabs

Had a picnic in the sun

Built a sandcastle

MY DAY OF NATURE DISCOVERIES

Match up stickers to what you saw at the shore
or would like to see on your next visit.

Discovered driftwood

Counted different kinds of seaweed

Found a jellyfish

Saw some fish

Did you see anything big?

What I Love about the Beach

Use this page to make a scene with stickers or to draw a picture of your favorite thing about being at the beach.

MY BEACH LOG

Make a keepsake of your day at the beach! Pull out this sheet and use a pencil and stickers to fill in both sides.

My Name:_____

The Beach I Visited:_____

The Date:_____

WEATHER REPORT

| SUNNY | RAINY | CLOUDY | WINDY |

The Beach Was...

Draw a picture or find some stickers that match your beach. Was it sandy or rocky? Was the wind blowing? What color was the water? Were there dunes with grasses and flowers?

What kinds of **PLANTS** do you see?

Beach rose

Sandwort

Sea rocket

Sand verbena

Can you find a ground cover plant that grows low along the sand?

Beach morning glory

American beachgrass

What sound does the wind make as it blows through the grass?

Seaside goldenrod

Beach evening primrose

Sea oats

Take a LOOK

Beach plants often have thick, waxy, or light-colored leaves. This kind of leaf holds water and reflects sunlight so the plants don't dry out.

OCEAN FOOD WEB

All living things have to eat to survive. Follow the colored arrows in the food chain diagram below to see what feeds what.

The **SUN** creates energy.

PLANTS and **ALGAE** use the sunlight to grow.

CLAMS, **CRABS**, and **JELLYFISH** eat small animals, zooplankton, and algae.

SMALL FISH and **BIRDS** eat vegetation and/or smaller sea creatures.

Some **LARGE FISH** and **MARINE MAMMALS** eat smaller animals. Some eat plants.

The mission of Storey Publishing is to serve our customers by
publishing practical information that encourages
personal independence in harmony with the environment.

Edited by Deanna F. Cook and Lisa H. Hiley
Art direction and book design by Jessica Armstrong
Text production by Erin Dawson and Jennifer Jepson Smith

Cover and interior illustrations by © Oana Befort
Interior photography by © Winky Lewis

Text © 2019 by Storey Publishing, LLC.

Storey Publishing
210 MASS MoCA Way
North Adams, MA 01247
storey.com

Printed in China by R.R. Donnelley
10 9 8 7 6 5 4 3 2 1

Library of Congress Cataloging-in-Publication Data on file